What Me Happy?

By Alison Blank

Scott Foresman
is an imprint of

Glenview, Illinois • Boston, Massachusetts • Chandler, Arizona •
Upper Saddle River, New Jersey

Jumping makes me happy.

Singing makes me happy.

Swimming makes me happy.

Painting makes me happy.

Eating makes me happy.

Helping makes me happy.

Hugging makes me happy.